PRESENTED TO

_____

Your kindness has made a difference that
will be remembered for eternity.

FROM

_____

Sister Eternal

To my beloved grandchildren: Daniel, Patrick, Eric, Jasmin, and Robin

—Dieter F. Uchtdorf

For my wife, Connie, with love. Thank you.

—Ben Sowards

Text © 2005 Dieter F. Uchtdorf
Illustrations © 2005 Ben Sowards

Visit us at deseretbook.com

Library of Congress Cataloging-in-Publication Data
Uchtdorf, Dieter F.
  Sister Eternal / Dieter F. Uchtdorf ; illustrated by Ben Sowards.
    p. cm.
  ISBN 1-59038-535-7 (hardcover : alk. paper)
  1. Uchtdorf, Dieter F. 2. Mormon Church—Apostles—Biography. 3. Church
of Jesus Christ of Latter-day Saints—Apostles—Biography. I. Title.
  BX8695.U32A3 2005
  289.3'092—dc22   2005018990

Printed in Mexico   18961
R. R. Donnelley and Sons, Reynosa, Mexico
10   9   8   7   6   5   4   3   2   1

Sister Eternal

A True Story Told by

DIETER F. UCHTDORF

ILLUSTRATED BY BEN SOWARDS

DESERET
BOOK

SALT LAKE CITY, UTAH

When I think of the people who have shaped my life, I am deeply grateful for the wonderful influence of faithful daughters of God. An experience in my early childhood with one such woman put our family on a course that will have eternal consequences.

oward the end of World War II, my father was drafted into the German army and sent to the western front of the war, leaving my mother alone to care for our family. As the fighting moved from Russia toward our town in Czechoslovakia, we heard rumors about terrible things being suffered by those in the way of the advancing armies. My mother decided we should flee to Germany, where her parents were living.

We were on one of the last refugee trains heading westward, and the journey, which normally would have taken one or two days, took us almost two weeks. During that time, we were cold and hungry and afraid. We were in a war zone, and the train was often stopped due to attacking aircraft or blocked railroad tracks.

*A*long the way, kind people brought food and other supplies to the stations where we stopped. One night my mother stepped out of the passenger car to try to find some food for her four children. When she returned, to her great horror, the train with her children on it was gone!

$\mathcal{F}$rantic with worry, she prayed on the deserted track for heavenly help. After praying, she felt to search all around the large train station. Finally, to her relief, she found our train, which had been moved to another track after she stepped out to gather food for us. We were grateful to have felt God's protection and guidance to keep our family together when so many others were separated from their loved ones.

$\mathcal{U}$nder the determined leadership of my mother, we reached her hometown and were reunited with her parents in Zwickau, East Germany. There were frequent nighttime air raids at the time, and I recall going to a bomb shelter on a hill, some distance from our home. Those hurried walks were often illuminated by what we children called "Christmas Trees"—glowing bombs dropped in advance of the attackers to help them see their targets. We always felt joy when we returned after a raid to find our house still standing.

During those dark and dangerous times it was a constant challenge to find basic needs such as food, clothing, and shelter. Standing in long lines, waiting for food or coal, was part of everyday life. Whenever we heard that something might be available, a member of the family would get in line as a placeholder, not knowing for certain what kind of goods might be offered.

One day, my grandmother, Auguste Opelt, was standing in such a line, and as usual she was talking with the person next to her. That day, that person was a friendly, elderly, white-haired lady who invited my grandmother to come with her to her church services on Sunday.

$\mathcal{M}$y grandmother was a Lutheran, but she had always been interested in religion and had even explored some other churches. She immediately liked this kindly woman who identified herself as a member of The Church of Jesus Christ of Latter-day Saints and who spoke so openly and confidently about her religion.

The following Sunday, my grandmother invited my parents to join her in attending this new church. We did not go with our parents because they felt it would be inappropriate to show up with four lively children the first time. This impression quickly changed, however, when they arrived to find the room filled to capacity with people of all ages. From that day on, we all went to church with the Latter-day Saints.

*W*e met in those days in a cold, cramped, rented back room. The electricity often failed, but the light of the message of the restored gospel was there in great abundance. Surrounded by the love, friendship, and helping hands of the members, we learned and grew in our testimonies. Eventually all the members of my family were baptized, though I had to wait two years, until I turned eight, to receive that blessing, which took place in an indoor, public swimming pool.

In the years following the war, through a distribution system overseen by Elder Ezra Taft Benson, the Church provided much-needed clothing, food, and other supplies for the Saints living in war-torn Europe. As newly baptized members of the Church, my parents were reluctant to accept any of these goods, but they eventually did, and I can still remember the taste of wheat and canned peaches, which we ate in our home, thanking God for the love and generosity of our brothers and sisters in the United States who had donated these life-saving goods for their previous enemies.

After this time of darkness, fear, and disaster, light came back into our lives because of the gospel and our membership in the restored Church of Jesus Christ. All this was made possible for us by a wonderful, angel-like sister who was courageous enough to invite my grandmother to come to church. Her act of kindness, though it may have seemed small at the time, changed all of our lives forever.

How grateful I am for her! How grateful my children and grandchildren are for her! To my knowledge, she had no family of her own, but we consider her part of our family. She has been and always will be a blessing to us. Interestingly enough, this elderly, single sister's name is *Ewig*, which translates into English as "Sister Eternal."